November 27, 1983

Dear Nik & Sandy;

To two people who have grown to love Korea as we do. We will miss you!

Love

Jim & Lois

KOREA

In olden times, men found a symbol for everything in the qualities
   of jade.
It stands for benevolence, because it is soft to the touch, smooth and
   caressing;
For Prudence, because it is fine-grained, subtle, and firm;
For Justice, because it has edges but injures not;
For Courtesy, because it descends to the ground when hung from
   the belt as an ornament;
For Music, because it responds to percussive sound with a clear,
   high, prolonged tone, then suddenly finishes;
For Loyalty, because its flaws are not concealed by its brilliance,
   nor its brilliance by its flaws;
For Sincerity, because it shows itself as it is, from whatever side one
   may view it;
For Heaven, because its fogginess is like the iridescence of clouds;
For Earth, because its essence appears in mountains and rivers;
For Valor, because when formed as scepters and tablets, it is the
   emblem of princely dignity;
For the True Way, because there is no one under the sun who does
   not value it.
It is said, in the Book of Verse: "I think of my lord, who is as sweet
   as jade."
This is why the sages of old made much of jade.

Confucius, *Notes on Manners and Ceremonies* (LI KI XLV, 13)

KOREA

Jean-Claude and Roland Michaud

With 85 colour illustrations and 1 map

 Thames and Hudson

Translated from the French by Alexis Gregory

First published in Great Britain in 1981
by Thames and Hudson Ltd. London
English translation © 1981 Thames and Hudson Ltd. London
and The Vendome Press, New York

© 1981 Sté Nlle des Éditions du Chêne, Paris

Printed in Switzerland and bound in France

4

Korea in History: An Editorial Note

Korea is a peninsular, largely mountainous land bounded on the west by Korea Bay (an arm of the Yellow Sea), on the south by Korea Strait and the Yellow Sea, and on the east by the Sea of Japan. In the north the Yalu and Tumen rivers mark the boundaries between Korea and its neighbors, China and the USSR. The country's climate ranges from extremely dry, cold winters in the north to almost tropical conditions in parts of the south.

Owing to the brutal Korean War of 1950–53 and the internal division imposed by the infamous 38th Parallel, Korea's recent history is only too familiar. But this story comes to seem all the more poignant in the light of the long traditions of culture and civilization—traditions of learning, piety, a profound sense of nationhood, and gradual but progressive liberalization—going all the way back to the 12th century B.C., when a Chinese scholar founded a colony at Pyŏngyang among the North Asian tribes from which the Koreans descend. Like China, post-Iron-Age Korea developed an agricultural economy. And from China Korea absorbed that nation's written characters, laws and decrees, Confucianism and painting. Still, Korea had its own language and invented its own alphabet, developed its own way of life, and improved upon all its borrowings to suit its own needs.

The first native state, Koguryŏ, arose near the Yalu River around A.D. 100, and by the 4th century it had conquered the Chinese outposts farther south. Also emerging in the south were two new Korean kingdoms, Paekche (c. 250 A.D.) and the powerful state of Silla (c. 350 A.D.). Supported by China, Silla overpowered Koguryŏ and Paekche in the 7th century and unified the peninsula under its single rule. Now Korea prospered, governed by monarchy, a landed aristocracy, and a professional civil service, all of which permitted the royal house to build palaces and tombs on an elaborate and extravagant scale. It was at this time that Koreans accepted Buddhism from China, which became a nationalistic religion praying for the protection and welfare of the state. The flowering of official Buddhism produced many beautiful temples and great works of art. The Zen branch of the system also emerged at this time, with its stress upon the importance of realizing, through contemplation, the inborn Buddha nature of each individual.

By 918 general unrest among the underprivileged of Korean society caused the rise of Koryŏ (whence the name Korea) and its slightly more flexible and responsive government. Deeply Buddhist in character, the regime built grand temples, where the faithful could observe rituals and pray for the prosperity of the nation. Korean Buddhism, mixed with Taoist geomancy and the yin-yang theory of opposites (in which earthly and heavenly cosmic forces were seen in various forms of relationship), reached its climax, dominating both the court and the populace. But Confucianism, another import from China, flourished, especially on the academic level.

A time of trouble began in the 12th century, characterized by peasant rebellions, military coups and repression, the retreat of Buddhism into the mountains, and, finally, the Mongol invasion of 1231. Koreans reacted to the nomadic intruders by turning out highly advanced poems and natural history books to demonstrate their national and cultural superiority. It was now that Korean monks carved the 81, 137 blocks of the Korean *Tripitaka* at the exile capital on Kanghwa Island, the effort designed to win back Buddha's protection against the oppressors.

In 1392 the Yi Dynasty entered upon its long reign in Korea, producing twenty-six monarchs and lasting until 1910. The Yi made Seoul their capital and ethical Confucianism the state religion. Korean culture blossomed as never before, especially in the reign of Sejong the Great. It yielded movable type in 1234 and many publications in medicine, astronomy, geography, history, agriculture, and, in 1443, a complete Korean phonetic alphabet. Late in the 15th century, Korean scholars made significant contributions to the theoretical refinement of Confucianism.

In the late 16th century, Korea, aided by Ming China and even by its own Buddhist priests, repulsed an invasion launched from Japan. The defense proved successful, but only after the conflict had laid waste to much of the peninsula and its great heritage of royal and religious treasures. Some scholars and artisans found themselves kidnapped into Japan and there forced to teach Korea's more advanced technology.

The 17th and 18th centuries brought important changes to Korea. Rice transplantation and improved irrigation became basic to agriculture. This, plus the cultivation of such special crops as tobacco and ginseng, resulted not only in higher living standards for agrarian workers but also in expanded trade and commerce for urban dwellers. Now scholarship shifted from traditional theorizing to issues more related to the practical needs of society and the nation. Comparable trends developed in arts and letters, producing not only popular works but even works of social protest.

The period also witnessed the arrival of influences from Europe, beginning with a Dutch ship that went aground on Korean shores in 1656. From this contact came the first book ever published on Korea in the West. Along with the merchants and traders appeared Western science and the missionary priests of the Catholic Church. Confucianists had little difficulty embracing the ethical content of Christianity. Most of the early converts were aristocratic scholars, but commoners too came to accept the doctrine of equality of all men before God and a new joy in the Christian belief in life after death. Eventually, however, Catholic condemnation of Confucian ancestor worship as pure idolatry brought retaliation from the Korean government. In the 19th century Protestantism also found a following in Korea, and the general spread of missionary instruction in Western thought imbued the Koreans with a strongly democratic spirit.

But for all its liberalizations, modern Korea suffered great turmoil throughout the 19th century. During the minority of ruling princes, maternal relatives seized power and brought the government to the verge of collapse, with one peasant uprising succeeding another. In keeping with their native propensity, many Koreans sought refuge in religion, which produced *Tonghak* ("Eastern Learning"), as opposed to *Sŏhak* ("Western Learning"—that is, Catholicism), a religion whose animism held great appeal for agrarian Korea. An anti-Western movement indigenous to Korea, Tonghak syncretized Taoism, Confucianism, and Buddhism, stressing social action and the principle that God and man are one.

Further attempts to penetrate Korea for commerical purposes brought the burning of the USS *General Sherman* and a domestic upheaval that gave Japan its opportunity. Japanese influence aroused Ch'ing China, which forced Korea to sign a treaty favorable to Chinese merchants. Soon, however, Great Britain, the United States, Russia, and France all succeeded in gaining trade arrangements in Korea. With their traditions of learning and technical innovation, Koreans quickly developed Western-style schools, newspapers, and increasingly liberal thought. More revolts ensued, leading to war with Japan in 1894, which ended with the defeat of Korea and a series of Japanese-dictated reforms. The success of Japan and its subsequent seizure in Manchuria were more than Russia could tolerate. But when Japan won the Russo-Japanese War of 1904–05, the Treaty of Portsmouth recognized Japan's undisputed supremacy in Korea. In 1910 Japan annexed Korea, ending the centuries-old Yi Dynasty.

Japan built modern industries and railroads, but failed to stifle Korean longing for freedom. After 1919 a provisional government under Syngman Rhee was established in Shanghai. At the Cairo Conference in 1943, the wartime Allies—Great Britain, the United States, and China—promised Korea independence. Following the Japanese capitulation, the country was arbitrarily divided into two occupation zones, with the Russians north and the Americans south of the line of lateral 38°N. As relations between the occupying powers worsened, trade ceased between the industrial north and the agrarian south, creating immense hardship for the Korean people. But in 1948 the division was formalized when two separate regimes—North Korea and South Korea—were established. In June 1950, after the withdrawal of all occupying forces, the North Korean army launched a surprise attack on South Korea, thereby precipitating the Korean War and all that has ensued for a distinguished and now much-afflicted nation.

Still, the Koreans retain their deeply religious and mystical nature, and nowhere is this more evident than in the vigorous survival of shamanism, a folk tradition that can be traced back to the primeval genesis of Korean society. According to shamanist belief, the visible world is pervaded by invisible forces or spirits that affect the lives of the living. The role of the shaman is to shield humanity from these spirits by coming into contact with the mysterious spirit world and rendering its destructive power harmless. By supernatural or mediumistic means, the shaman (frequently a woman) is supposed to control and manipulate nature. The animism inherent in the shamanist system has made it particularly tenacious among the country and village population.

Another symptom of the abiding spirituality of Korean civilization is the decision, made in 1905, to rename Tonghak, which its gentle adherents now call *Ch'ondogyo,* or the religion of the "Heavenly Way."

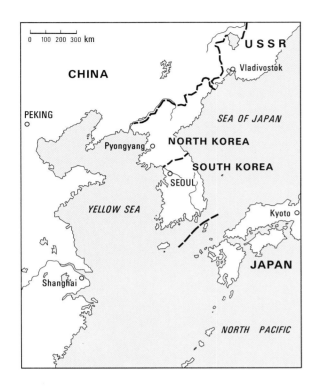

The Diamond Mountains

Detail of a folding screen (8 panels) representing the Diamond Mountains. Yi Dynasty (Zo-Za-Yong Collection. Emille Museum. Seoul).

On the fifteenth day of the first month of the lunar year, the full moon sheds white beams upon the frozen river and diffuses an ashen light among the naked branches of maples and beeches. Frost powders the Snow Mountains. Anxious about the crunch of our steps on the fragile surface of blue abysses, we have entered a valley that, as far as the eye can see, looks like a folding screen with a thousand panels. Below us, the flowing torrent gurgles under a shell of ice. For me, the Chinese name for these places contains more poetry than anything I could possibly express or describe: the Great Cerulean Peak, the Valley of the Nine Abysses, the Snow Mountains. The peaks soar, the water rushes, the snow falls. And I have only a pencil with which to tell of such things!

Chinese ideograms make everything more beautiful: rocks, inns, and villages. They derive a celestial essence from each object and endow it with a poetic aura. Through them, a magical transmutation occurs: the rock of ordinary granite assumes the character of jade; the country inn appears as a palace. The Chinese character is an image that reduces the denoted object to its archetype. The mountain becomes a trio of peaks; the island, a bird on the mountain; the bird, a crested head and ruffled feathers. Writing is calligraphy. Ink and paper alone can overwhelm my spirit.

Sir Yang had a small pavilion built in the heart of these mountains. Known as a provincial governor, he also enjoyed great respect for the dragon style of his calligraphy. He christened his pavilion *pi rae jōng*—three characters signifying "the pavilion reached by flying." Once the house was finished, Yang took a special brush made of whale whiskers and formed the lovely character *pi* ("to fly") in a flourish of feathers and wings. The result was so perfect that he did not dare go on, fearing the remainder might be less than the beginning. This is why the emblem started and finished with a single character: *pi*. Some years later, a terrible hurricane blew through this peaceful place and swept the famous sign up into the clouds. At that very moment Yang Bongnae died at a location far away from his beloved pavilion. The year was 1584, when this happened in the Diamond Mountains.

Alas, the Diamond Mountains are inaccessible to us today, situated north of the 38th Parallel that cuts Korea in half. Still, we must try to evoke them, for otherwise the soul of this country would certainly elude our grasp. Moreover, the Snow Mountains, into which our sure-footed friend Jai Yŏng is guiding us, are sometimes called the "Little Diamond Mountains," because of the foretaste they give of the twelve thousand rocky peaks to be found farther north.

The now-remote Diamond Mountains have inspired a very singular type of landscape painting. Here a mountain appears as a living, breathing form. It is the spirit of the mountain that has been represented. Water of a mirror-like stillness becomes a flux; rock, a frozen flame or a phantom. Meanwhile, the monastery with its pagoda roof seems to dance like a frail skiff in the trough of waves generated by that ocean of forces. This is a fantastic art. It metamorphoses peaks into thousands of enigmatic penitents, their heads covered with pointed cowls. Even the folds in the steep terrain resemble the drapery of a monk's habit, the hood disclosing, not a face, but the nestled image of a temple, complete with miniature garden. Elsewhere, the mountains assume the crystalline forms of cubes. Caught in a morning light, these adamantine crests provide an unforgettable vision. The landscape makes one think of a cosmic choir, so much do the crystal rocks seem like musical instruments, struck by water to draw forth a strange melody.

When Kim Satkat, 19th-century Korea's rain-hatted wandering poet, first came upon the Diamond Mountains, he forgot all the learning he had acquired throughout his life. The more he penetrated this mysterious nature, the more he became like a child, mumbling a sort of ditty (in which *bong* means "peak"):

> *One* bong, *two* bong, *three four* bong,
> *Five* bong, *six* bong, *seven eight* bong.

Whenever hunger overtook him, Kim Satkat would knock on the door of a Buddhist monastery, hoping for a free meal. One snowy evening, an old monk responded. Taking the poet for a beggar, he scowled and turned a cold shoulder. Finally, sensing the presence of an artist, the monk decided to test him in a poetry competition:

The monk:	*White of moon,*
	White of snow,
	White of sky,
	White of earth.
The poet:	*Deep the peak,*
	Deep the water,
	Deep the breath
	Of the passing guest.

It is to Mr. Zozayong, a great lover of painting and the perfect exemplar of the Korean spirit, that we owe the story of calligraphy and the calligraphy of the poet.

The Melancholic Island

The Melancholic Island is situated in the Sea of Japan. A black volcanic rock, it is totally inhospitable, a foggy realm floating on an ocean of impermanence and lashed by the waves of time. It opens into dark grottoes and bristles with juniper-sprouting rocks. At the same time that fairies cast their flowers, the gods of the volcanoes rained down their ashes. Ah, if only we could have had the heart of the red camelia that flowered under the snow, how tenderly we would have loved it!

The island's inhabitants gather medicinal herbs that taste like leeks. Squid, called *o-jingō,* dangle laconically from clotheslines, limp as old rags. In the narrow, winding streets of the port, we can see a scattering of umbrellas struggling against gusts of wind, just as in Japanese prints.

In the coffee shop where we take shelter, two waitresses—one in a long dress and the other in jeans—make charming replacements for the boys in the café at our lodging.

We savor the delicious Drink of Seven Flavors in which bits of cinnamon float about an island of egg yolk. A comforting warmth radiates from a stove fed with the usual twenty-two-hole cylinders of coal.

Meanwhile, we find ourselves plied with pop music and old tales. Outside, the raucous voice of a neighboring church bell adds to the cacophony.

"Must our world be so spoiled?" seems to be the question posed by a plaster head that peers down at us, its features undoubtedly those of a Brutus or a Cassius.

"But where are we anyway?" the bell would appear to ask. "Really, you aren't there at all! Say 'Tong-do,' and you will have it right." We are in Tong-do, the capital of the Melancholic Island.

To go from there to the mainland, it takes ten hours by an old tub, which casts us—more dead than alive—onto the dock at Pohang.

We had dreamed of a paradise island in the Sea of Japan. And, following our visit to the Confucian School of the Jade Mountain, then to the Precious Mirror Buddhist monastery, we decided to join a student-poet and go as Taoist pilgrims to Ullūng-do. We had once read the Chinese philosopher Tchouang-tse, who said: "On the distant island of Kou-chee live transcendent men, white as snow, fresh as babes, who take no food but merely breathe the air and drink the dew. They travel through space, with clouds as chariots and dragons as steeds." This nourished our reveries.

Unfortunately, we had not bothered to look up the meaning of *Ul.* It is in fact one of the most complicated of Chinese characters, one that signifies the somber and the melancholy. Ullūng-do translates literally as "Island of the Dark Mountain." And the island turned out to be indeed black, thanks to its volcanic origins. But with the snow falling, we saw it as white. Once the place was actually called "Mountain of Feathers," and even now many allusions to winged spirits—the immortal beings of the Taoist tradition—survive in the names of places.

Be that as it may, we retain a cruel memory of this wintry island, where we had to wade in mud and snow from To-dong to Jō-dong, as if from Charybdis to Scylla. This was our Melancholic Island! It is with regret that we speak of it—and even more of ourselves:

Thus the mariner, searching for treasures of old,
Brings back salty herring in lieu of gold.

The Village of the Blue Crane

The inhabitants of Blue Crane find their food tasty, think their dress elegant, take delight in the coziness of their homes, and believe their yoke and burden to be light and easy. This is an enchanting village, where everyone has always sung "The Eternal Middle Path" and where *The Book of the True Way and of Virtue,* that Taoist mixture of wise words and utopian dicta, has been preserved like a strange and wondrous music.

Lao-tse said: "If I were the prince of a small state, I would devote myself to making my subjects fear death, so that they would not dare take up armor and lance, or board either boat or chariot. Even if they heard the cock crow or the dog bark in a neighboring village, they would have neither the desire nor the temerity to go and investigate. They would die of old age without ever having left my principality."

Every day the villagers perform their rites. They call their religion the "Heavenly Way." It is founded on the triple doctrine of Confucius, the Master of Courtesy; Lao-tse, the Juvenile Ancient (meaning wise man or philosopher); and Buddha, the Great Hero.

By the delicacy and purity of their manners, the villagers evoke the "Fresh Morning"—that is, the period of the Yi Dynasty, which had succeeded in the kingdom of Koryō (whence "Korea") and revived the ancient name of "Calm Morning."

The villagers all wear their finery with the artfulness of swans. The men dress in hats of black horsehair that give them an aristocratic charm. Underneath, their own long hair is gathered up in a bun on the top of the head. Bare-headed youths still, as of old, plait their tresses in long pigtails.

A visit to the village school takes us into the heart of old Korea. Here the male children learn to read and write Chinese characters and the Korean alphabet, the latter a legacy from wise King Sejong, a monarch of the 15th century.

Dressed in traditional robes, the youngsters sit on the plank floor, which is comfortably heated by a hearth below. Their voices monotone, they recite from the canonical books, swaying back and forth on their haunches to the rhythm of the chant. They follow the writing with the aid of a meticulously decorated wand and count the repetitions on a sort of rosary made of paper. Their ABC is called *The Classic of One Thousand Characters,* the history of which deserves telling.

One chronicle reports that a Chinese Emperor named Wou-ti, having drawn a thousand characters on loose sheets, gave them one day to his minister with the instruction that he make them into a poem. This took place in the 6th century. The task was completed in one night, but it exacted such an effort that the poet emerged the next morning with white hair. Thus, the volume he wrote is called *The Book of the White-Haired Man.* Proceeding in orderly fashion from Heaven to Earth and then to Man, this long poem gathers the universe into a series of verses each of which opens with a pair of well-known lines:

> *Heaven and Earth, Dark and Light,*
> *Space and Time, fallow immensity.*

Like a bottomless treasure chest, this text has never ceased to provide names for places, *noms de plume,* maxims, and proverbs, such as the one that captures the schoolboy's despair:

> *Heaven Earth, Dark Light,*
> *Three years to master these four characters....*
> *When will I get to the end?*

Also among the books used by the pupils is a moral treatise designed to teach filial piety. Here we find: "Between Heaven and Earth there are ten thousand creatures, but only man is honorable. He is honorable because he possesses the Five Relationships. For this reason, Mencius has said there should be:

> *Intimacy between father and son*
> *Justice between prince and subject*
> *Distinction between husband and wife*
> *Precedence between older and younger*
> *And good faith between friends.*

Our thin-bearded host and guide is an amiable and cultivated grandfather. His creased face behind round eyeglasses seems to radiate light like a precious stone. An agreeable smile lifts both corners of his mouth, while an aura of exquisite courtesy emanates from his gestures and reverential bow, all of which transforms a country fellow into a gentleman. The Chinese used to refer to Korea as "the nation of courteous gentlemen."

Breezes scatter the petals of early April throughout the orchards. Just as in *The Tale of the Origin of Fishing* by Tao Yuan-ming, the poet of the stringless lute, we discover a small community so completely isolated from the world that it has been able to preserve the usages and customs of a distant age.

The villagers offer us honey from their hives and take us on a picnic among rocks and pines. A dappling spring light falls through the bamboo shoots. *Kwong,* the pheasant, taken by surprise, leaps out of the thicket and ascends with all his colors in heavy flight. Bounding from stone to stone, then suddenly still, *Daramjui,* the striped-back squirrel, casts a keen eye on the beans set out for our meal. *Kegouri,* the frog, moss-colored on top and cinnabar below, appears to be meditating on the bank of a stream. Suddenly plop! and he is upside down.

Those who gather herbs fan out to unearth the original root stock of pines and to harvest simples. These growths with their precious juices suck at the very breast of the earth. In tearing the roots from the lap of their mother, the forager deprives them of their life in order to suck the sap and thus extract nature's goodness. *Atractylis lancea, Pachyma cocos, Panax ginseng*—these capitulated, or "flower-headed," ladies, these ascomycete truffles, these princley *Araliacede* whose dynasty can be traced back to tertiary times, an age they shared with creatures now long extinct—this is what stimulates the gatherer of medicinal herbs. He knows the spirit of the valley and immerses himself in the deep matrix of the earth.

> *The spirit of the valley never dies,*
> *It is called the mysterious female;*
> *The entrance to the mysterious female*
> *Is called the root of Heaven and Earth.*

There the herb gatherer sometimes collects the antlers of the hart-flower held in the lakes of the melliferous woodbine, and sometimes he seeks the elusive root of life. Unless, of course, deprived of the purity of heart which alone makes capture possible, he goes off and steals from the ginseng merchant. In the jargon of earlier brigandage, the ambushes mounted against the Chinese dressed in blue cotton were called "pheasant hunts," while "swan hunt" designated the pursuit of white-clad Koreans.

Ginseng is the Koreans' *pullocho,* the herb of eternal youth—or, at least, the closest thing to it available here below. The Chinese ideogram for "life" resembles a growing plant, but a plant in the form of a man. Thus, like a pun, the growing-plant-shaped-like-a-man comes to mean "human life." Here, the mountaineer who drinks only from the purest springs, and whose spirit moves easily through the forest of symbols, sees a felicitous expression of the

"signature" theory, which holds that through its visible aspect a plant discloses its curative virtues.

The root of life, born of and nourished by the conjunction of Heaven and Earth, contains a power that mysteriously harmonizes with human life. Along with sun and snow, water and rock, pine and bamboo, the speckled stag, the tortoise, and the blue crane, it numbers among the ten symbols of long life. The sky-colored crane—what could this be but a mount for immortals?

Now that I dream of the Village of the Blue Crane, a song comes back to me from the distant past:

> *When the fresh breeze blows*
> *From the land of your birth*
> *To my senses there flows*
> *A wind of Paradise on Earth.*

The Scholar

Here is the scholar in a coat whose periwinkle color is intensified by the white of an immaculate collar. Coming forward from the door of his house, he invites us inside. As his slippers touch the steps leading to the humble cottage, they seem like two white notes in a bar of music for which the wearer would be the clef. His hair is gray, his cheekbones prominent, his face thin, his eyes gentle and lively. Occasionally a bittersweet smile breaks into measured laughter.

Neither the impromptu character of our visit, nor our insistence upon having his calligraphic instruments put on the writing table disturbs the tranquility of this sage.

He pours water and steadies his hand on the ink stick in order to rub it circular fashion on the moistened stone. Then, merely by balancing from the shoulder, without any pressure from the palm of his hand, he makes his brush produce a series of nine perfect characters. The words are inscribed as if in a magic square. For it to make sense in a Western language, we have no choice but to break this string of pearls:

To be awakened by Poetry
To be supported by Ritual
To be perfected by Music.

This sentence, says the master, summarizes the contents of the Four Books.

Putting down his brush, the calligrapher takes the seal, presses it hard into the corner of the stuffing box, and then, at the bottom of his writing, prints an angular red mark—fire or blood.

A calabash hung on the wall, along with a flyswatter, a theatrical mask, a brush made of thick bamboo and gray wolf's hair, joins the golden light filtering through the window to surround the master with an atmosphere of mystery.

Through the half-open door leading to the next room, we hear the sound of boiling tea. Meanwhile, across the fields of ginseng comes the voice of a disciple entoning the sacred books.

Corean Dignitary. Yi Dynasty.
(Etienne Sancho Collection).

13

Springtime Offering to Confucius

When the heavy wooden doors of Seoul's Sanctuary of Letters open to receive the spirits, they creak like something from beyond the tomb.

Dignitaries in their fine-spun headdresses, each arrangement run through with a large horizontal pin, wait at the foot of a high terrace fronting on the temple housing the Tablets of the Sages. Gray-bearded venerables in mineral-blue robes embroidered with the animal motifs of their various ranks carry the writing table on which the commandments are inscribed. They stand still and erect, leaning neither to the left nor to the right in order not to unbalance Heaven and Earth for which man is the pivot. When they prostrate themselves, they do it all at once and four times, the brow touching the ground and the right hand crossed by the celestial left. When they move into single file, the beads of jade hung from their belts regulate the proper measure of their steps.

The voice of an officiating priest can be heard pearling out Chinese sounds. The master of ceremonies, a small man in tulip red, gives him a brief direction from time to time, doing so with the single syllable for: "Recite!"

The ceremony enacted here has been observed in this precinct since 1398, twice a year, in spring and in autumn. It is an ancient legacy of the ritual practiced by the earliest dynasties, a ritual that has now totally disappeared in China, where it originated. The purpose is to gather and redirect the spirits of Confucius and his thirty-eight disciples, Chinese and Korean, after first offering them a tribute of silk and food.

A group of black-haired women students, all dressed in red garments across which sun and wind play as in the petals of a poppy, are aligned in a perfect square, eight rows to a side and facing south. A cord the color of bluets falls from every belt. The young women bend and sway, slowly like wheat responding to the wind. With a gentle movement, each girl lifts a foot shod in black felt and, turning first to the east, then to the west and the north, bends again.

Square black caps and round red ones are put on alternately according to the sequence of civil or military dances. For the former the ladies wield a flute and a dragon head. For the latter, they strike a symbolic ax against a wooden shield, doing so with a rhythm whose reverberations are meant to sow fear.

Here everything is order and beauty, and meant to represent the whole universe: Heaven and Earth, peace and war, fire and water, cardinal numbers and points.

But I much prefer the nonchalance of the schoolgirls who, in the back courtyard, cannot help giggling as they practice this solemn ritual. Rather than obedient spears of wheat, they are more like wildflowers tossing in the wind.

An orchestra costumed in a rose similar to that of the Royal Azalea, rows of nobles wearing gowns of strong violet reminiscent of bougainvillea, phalanxes of scholars in white coats, coiffed in caps of black horsehair the weave of which creates a beautiful moiré pattern—in all, a spectacle that mere words cannot describe. And how could verbal language re-create the sounds that come from the sonorous stones, sounds without parallel in my experience, slowly, slowly drawn not only from stone but also from metal, wood, hide, silk, and, hardly less strange to my ears, the human voice. At a high pitch the voices recall the sparrow hawk soaring into flight; lower, they make one think of fish diving into the depths. Then, too, they seem as slow as constellations circling about a pole and as pure as clear water falling from stone to stone in silvery, crystalline notes.

This liturgy harmonizes our very breathing with timeless rhythms and places our hearts in a sacred place where, between Heaven and Earth, they expand to the dimensions of the universe.

Yin and Yang

"Seek knowledge, all the way to China." Thus spoke the Prophet of Islam, we are told, and the saying provides the motive for our trip to Korea. There we meet scholars, doctors, professors, the erudite, and the wise. We examine museum objects and pages of books. The response to every question is the same wherever we look: *yin* and *yang*. But what is this yin, this yang?

Yin and yang elude definition, even when evoked in terms of fire and water or sun and moon. There is no simple explanation of either yin or yang. From the start, we must mix a bit of fire with the snow and a bit of water with the wine, if we are to have any understanding of whatever yin and yang may mean. Against the red glow of the sun the crow stands on three legs, cold and black. In the chill light of the moon the warm-furred rabbit or hare crunches on cinnamon bark to prepare the *elixir vitae,* all of which reminds us of a jingle learned in childhood.

> *I saw in the moon* (yin)
> *Three little rabbits* (yang)
> *Who were eating prunes* (yin)
> *Like little rascals* (yang)
> *Pipe in their mouth* (yin)
> *Glass in their hand* (yang)
> *Saying, Ladies* (yin)
> *Pour some wine* (yang)
> *To the top.*

In pointing out the yin or the yang of each allusion, we have wanted to demonstrate the Oriental perfection of the ditty.

The Book of a Thousand Characters, in which generations of Korean school children have stumbled their way through the Chinese language, says:

> *Gold* (yang) *comes from the waters* (yin) *of the River Li*
> *Jade* (yin) *comes from the Kun-Gang Mountains* (yang).

Yin and Yang are the point of departure for a strange symbolism founded, from the outset, upon a kind of ambivalence that is easier to illustrate on an emotional or affective level than to explain in rational terms. Yet, Père Amiot wrote from Peking in 1783 to Abbé Bertin: "These words [*yin* and *yang*] provide the key to every science." And he was right, in that geomancy, acupuncture, the Korean alphabet, indeed everything in China or Korea is yoked together like the two-horse chariot of yin and yang, which gradually became the algebra of Oriental science.

But before they were scholasticized, yin and yang belonged to the world of shamanism. The scholastic, like the Confucian, classifies, dividing the world into men and women, nobles and serfs, etc. The shaman, on the other hand, blends, confounds, fuses, synthesizes, transforms, and dissolves the rigidity of creation. He crosses barriers separating the various levels of being, accomplishes the Nocturnal Voyage (as a prophet or a shaman), and becomes a butterfly (like the poet-philosopher Tchouang-tse) or an otter, even a tiger. The *moudang* sometimes dresses as a man and sometimes as a woman; sometimes he prays and sometimes he laughs. The Confucian cuts the right off from the left. The shaman stitches them back together. He is both male and female. He passes through fire as if he were ice, yet without melting. His powers preexisted the flood, when our body was like a kernel enveloped in soul, when the world was still in flux, still gestating in the great crucible of nature.

The sanctuary door painted with the emblem of the "Great Summit," the court musician's ritual drum with its "whirling" image, the trigram on the monastery bell rung by an old guardian at dawn, and the *moudang*'s fan painted in the colors of yin and yang—all exist for the shamanist ear and eye. It is also the shaman who, in the kingdom that lies between sleeping and dreaming, sees the cold black crow in the red hot sun and the soft rabbit in the hard light of the moon.

But how, you may well ask, is it possible to base a science upon such nonsense? Certainly, if you look at the moon with a Galilean eye, the seated hare disappears. The ancients may not have been the founders of our precious "science." Instead, they had their "techniques" and their "arts," and indeed they may have got lost following the chiming sounds of yin and yang. But can we afford to say that someone who travels along a different path goes in the wrong direction? At the sources of yin and yang there may be a better wine to drink than in a whole barrel of our knowledge.

But the great lords
In horns and feathered hats
Fluttered like so many dreadful bats.
And the weasels, out of fright,
Fell into the most awful plight.

The Rice-Paddy Quartet

Dressed in bluebell-colored tunics hanging loosely over black trousers, their heads crowned with gray and gold miters, hoisting thin poles of bamboo like lances, and waving white flags embellished with trigrams and images of warriors and dragons, the standard-bearers march to a whine like bagpipes along the narrow ridge of rice-paddy dams.

A plow ox raises the dust in a distant rice field.

A quartet of musicians in single file, all dressed in white except for their black caps, play tunes, one with the babbling sounds of a reed, another with a soft-toned flute, a third with a strident trumpet, and the last with a drum, while their leader marches ahead clapping the rhythm with his hands.

A fat-fingered flute-player holds a tiny reed, his huge face swollen as if from blowing on this frail little wind instrument. The thin-faced drummer carries a drum shaped like an hourglass whose sound is deep or dry depending on which of its sides is struck, either with the palm of the hand or with a drumstick. The flute player handles his instrument with real authority, but his vibratos have long since been drowned out by the ear-splitting performance given by the trumpeter. At this point, the ensemble finds itself reflected upside down in the silvery mirror of a flooded rice field.

Venerables shod in half-boots and plumes appear on ponies decorated with pompoms of paper flowers. These, we are told, are generals. Confronted with such warriors from another age, how are we not to think of the battle between the weasels and the rats:

The Village Festival

We are at the local festival. Pop-eyed, Roland Michaud revels in the brightness of the costumes caught in the rain, all mixed with a scatter of umbrellas. Joining in a hunt for the white swan, he finds the rare bird. Now he thinks he has become Hokusai upon discovering a peddler carrying two buckets of water at either end of a pole, one the color of the sun, the other the color of the moon, and marching straight through the mud. Running, slipping, and almost falling, Roland follows. Just as the sun is eclipsed by a gathering fog, two matrons clad in duck blue suddenly appear. The artist rejoices at the chance to sketch them, but to gain better access to the fine beads sewn into their luminescent silk, he must separate the subjects from their neighbors. With this, he gets himself jostled, only to perceive, when countering aggression with a smile, that the gossips themselves make a perfect trio, their overall green attire entirely equal to the splendor of the blue ladies. This is how a crowd can provide a feast for the hungry photographer, often even in foul weather.

In front of the sanctuary of this little village, now turned into a sewer by the rain, several people are dancing about in the presence of the holy relics like so many marionettes. It seems like a real fracas. Within this musical din, a bell-mouth trumpet endlessly repeats the same four notes, always in a nasal timbre, struggling to dominate the gong and cymbal. Still warm, a sacrificial pig steams in its basin. On such an occasion, which comes every two years, a cord tied with two little paper ribbons is extended across the door of every home to ward off evil spirits.

Even so, at the center of this cacophony, the frog-men of television, who seem all the more froglike by virtue of their transparent rainwear, leap like toads into a pond and proceed to turn the place into a true frog pond, sullying the sanctuary, obscuring the rite, and throwing flashes of sacrilegious light onto the scene, all the while that, come midnight, the rain continues to fall and the wind to blow.

On the stoop of the sanctuary, a witch, her face as gray as an old potato, hums as she circles about a pole that is violently shaken by a trio of white-clad farmers. This is how the propitious spirit to whom the sacrifice has been offered responds.

Such a spectacle would be hard to endure were it not for the appearance of a lovely lass, some eighteen springs old, who, we are told, is the granddaughter of the old witch. With peaches in her cheeks, her eyes lowered on curly lashes, a tiny mouth made pale by the cold, this young *moudang* dances. Fluidly graceful and serene, she moves her arms like wings and turns in the midst of the hurly-burly as if it were not there. Meanwhile, the withered witch withdraws a few steps to blow her nose with her fingers.

It is just as well that they give us the grandmother's name in English: Plum, Young Lady! Since time, which deforms all, can change a plum into a prune, how could we be so shocked at the contrast between the old hag and the young beauty? As the poet says:

> *Is there a lady fair*
> *Whose beauty is always bold*
> *When time, sickness, and care*
> *Bring ugliness to her fold.*

This elderly woman who, with her prophecies and her dance, will tomorrow find ways to beguile the old of the village, while her skirts fill up with notes both large and small—I imagine her once not quite so ugly and quite capable of saying in her younger days:

> *Sweet and savage eyes*
> *Red and white cheeks*
> *Tender and loving words*
> *This is my magic circle.*

Musicians and dancer. Kim Hong Doh painting. XVIIIth century. (National Museum. Seoul).

17

The Enchantress

Golden Flower, originally from North Korea, is a *moudang*—some say a shaman. In this land, shamans usually are women. Ours is about thirty, slender and rather tall, and has the face of a squaw. Her eyes are like wind-rippled drops of dew in which black pearls glow. The corners of her wide mouth are ready to curl into a smile, albeit cloaked under a noble bearing.

The *kout*—the ceremony we are about to attend—is strictly a family affair. Except for us, all strangers and even neighbors are excluded.

A priestess kneeling before the consecrated food offering, praying as she rubs her palms together, a singer with a fan, a musician playing on bells, a sword dancer, a barefoot acrobat, a roguish, even ribald mime, an eloquent teller of endless tales, a resplendent princess, an exorcist with her green bows, a retiring nun, an oracle, magician, sometimes Circe and sometimes Pythia—the shaman is everything at once.

The ample sleeves of her organdy dress flutter like wings and fall to the floor. The black beans of an enormous chaplet play against the pines and cranes of her shoulder strap. The edges of her hood undulate under the breeze of her fan. And as she moves, is this the dance of a Korean queen or that of a Chinese king? Does she sing of sadness or of joy? Longing for her homeland. The voice is serene, a bewitching sound as it mixes with the chime of the seven bells in her earrings. Floating against her hip is a lovingly embroidered bag, into which an offering slips from time to time. Her eyes remain half-closed.

Without breaking the spell, Golden Flower changes her outer finery, as we watch her whole nature change. A moment ago she was a white butterfly, and now we see a spring flower. When she dons a robe of natural hemp and a straw hat, she could be a simple peasant. Then material shot with rainbow colors transforms her into a courtesan. Making up before a mirror, our beauty mimics a waking person, yawning, scratching, and stretching, to the great merriment of her audience. All this has accompaniment from hourglass-drum, gong, and cymbal, played by three elderly ladies crouching at her feet.

Out in the courtyard, the ceremony takes a different turn. There a black pig begins to scream as the sun sets. A mock hunt is staged with bow and arrow. Then, in proper sequence, the victim is castrated and, his throat slit, thrown dying into a basin of steaming water. Now everyone takes great pleasure in scraping the creature clean of his bristles. When finally skewered, this is no longer an animal but a bloodless object.

The carcass is borne on the prongs of a trident to the consecrated place. Posed in unstable balance upon a bowl turned upside down, the trident holds! This proves that the spirits have acknowledged the *kout*, and that fortune will smile upon all those gathered there.

Dawn in the Monastery

In the silence of the night, the heart of the monastery wakens to the hammering of the *moktak*, the musical block of wood that the watchman strikes as he goes from place to place singing a *sūtra*. As soon as the chant ceases, the bell of the great temple begins to swing its trigram under the blows of the ringer. Now the monks, torn from their sleep, crowd around basins of water to make their ablutions. Everything is gray, robes, sky, stones, walls—even the mountain, which seems as boneless as the meat of a *kalbi-tang*. But why do I have this taste for boiled beef in a community where eating meat is totally forbidden. Perhaps it is provoked by the bamboo fire which, sputtering at this hour, throws off a sweet smoke. Not far from here, the river flows by in a whisper, but no bird rises from its nest, or emits a cry.

Suddenly, the peace is broken by the deep sound of a drum, an enormous drum that a monk wielding a pair of sticks beats from the front and on all sides. Next, it is the great wooden fish that must suffer the wrath. Although fat, it has a hollow stomach into which the monk inserts his drumsticks and, like an enraged madman, raps away at the ribs. After the fish, the assailant takes his time before attacking the gong shaped like a cloud. Then, approaching the bell, he imitates the movements of a warrior. Under the shock of a battering ram that, after each assault, the monk must swing a bit to the side, since he cannot arrest its momentum all at once, the instrument sends out long reverberations, rumbling like thunder. But for all its boom, the bell hardly moves.

Twenty-eight claps of thunder rend the dawn. As the bell receives its final blow, the Temple of the Great Hero responds to the Pavilion of the Bell and Drum. Inside the temple and barely grazed with small, gentle taps, the bell marked with trigrams hums, then starts to swing under the growing impact of the mallet. The final volley, a blow struck with vigor, makes the primordial sound swell and subside in the very core of one's being.

The crescent moon pales, and the cherry blossoms become still whiter. In the forest the woodpecker echoes the *moktak* as it sets the rhythm for prayers. Dawn has come to the monastery.

The Hermitage of the Blue Lotus

The Vehicle of Diamond and Lightning (*Vajrayāna*) is a representative par excellence of the esoteric branch of Buddhism. Its vision derives from what a great contemporary master of the *sophia perennis* has called "the metaphysical transparency of the world," as well as from the purity of heart that renders this vision possible. The world and the heart are "empty," and in this emptiness radiates the light of Vajrayāna, the primordial Buddha, central and solitary. In the monasteries of Korea, the sanctuary consecrated to this cult is known as the Palace of the Light of the Great Void, since Light and Void constitute the adamantine substance of Vajrayāna. As for its fulgurant nature, this is to be found in methodology. Celestial in origin, Vajrayāna pierces with the irresistible force of lightning the more or less opaque layers of reality that its flashing light illuminates. Thus, it has the character of the *mantra*, that invocational formula whose subtle power is capable of breaking the hardened shell of the heart and that, by introducing therein the full resonance of the inner and outer Heaven, opens the heart to an influx of divinity.

These different levels of existence bear, according to the Reverend Master Yang Ik, the names of Earth, Water, Fire, Wind, Void, and Conscience. The method practiced by this monk, a master in martial arts, is not the *mantra*, but rather the *kūm-gang yŏng gwan*, "the adamantine spiritual vision." *Kūm-gang* means "diamond," but, by reference to the dual sense of the Sanskrit word *vajra*, for which *Kūm-gang* is the ideographic translation, the latter also connotes lightning. Consequently, the name of this martial art can just as well be translated as "the look with the power of a thunderbolt."

The master is drilling a small group of disciples in a remote hermitage—the Hermitage of the Blue Lotus. If lightning is related to fire and wind because it is the child of storm, and the diamond to the void and the illuminated conscience, the lotus corresponds to water and earth. It represents the passive and feminine pole—sweetness, compassion—just as the *vajra* symbolizes the active, virile pole, with its rigor and vacuity. Compassion and vacuity are the perfume and the light of Buddhism. Thus, the Hermitage of the Blue Lotus is a paradisiacal name for the exercise of a terrible art whose true purpose is not to smash the adversary with a thunderbolt but to obtain first, through the concentration of all energies, the perfect union of body and soul and then spiritual illumination. In this strange hermitage, Paradise resides in the shadow of swords, and the sword, if we may say so, falls under the shadow of Paradise.

But no sword is to be found on Master Bird (*Yank Ik* means "Two Wings"), nor on the disciples Tiger-of-Stone and Merciful Look—only simple raiment, eyes, and empty hands. These monks have the wind as their mount, a sharp gaze as their weapon, and the void as their ally.

The Old Tiger Man

"Streaks of clouds submitting to the solicitations of the wind," the spirit completely taken up with the cries of cicadas—now we are in the melancholy of autumn, on the "narrow point at the End of the World," near the Chestnut Hermitage. There are certain places where the patina of time has left no mark, and our pilgrimage recalls that of the poet Bashō who three centuries ago wandered through the Japanese Archipelago.

We locate the monk in the smoke-colored robe and ink-black hat who, bundle on his shoulder and gnarled stick in his hand, is happily preparing to leave the monastery at dawn, in an atmosphere redolent with the aroma of crushed pine branches. His name as a wandering monk is "Cloud and Water." A great walker, he bears under his kneecaps the traces of a thousand *moxas*. A tradition handed down for a millennium holds that these cauterizations strengthen vitality and thus should be practiced in preparation for long excursions. "I mended my torn trousers, changed the cord on my hat, and applied the *moxa* under my kneecaps, by the light of the moon on the Isle of Pines; the spirit already overflowing, I was relinquishing my abode to another," wrote Bashō.

Here the waters of the spring have collected in an empty tree trunk. The site also provides pine faggots, a thicket of bamboo with dried leaves, and the Pavilion of the Spirit of the Mountain. Spreading out from the entrance to the pavilion is a vast landscape of ridges and ravines. Russet ferns, blue pines, and the faded gold of a chestnut grove clothe the mountain in a mantle of brocade. The round-tile roofs of the many hermitages embroider the scene with a dragon's image.

Another dragon, this one with a beetling brow, appears on the east wall of the pavilion, while the west wall displays a tiger. Two emblems of east and west, they have been half-effaced by the weather. Under the sheltering porch the lotus flowers in an eternal springtime. A cool, light sound, as vague as the flight of a butterfly and, like it, carried by the wind, descends from the corner of a roof raised like a threatening horn against the evil spirits of the air. Here we spy a small aolian bell that a metal fish causes to tinkle sweetly.

We pass through a door made of wood latticework covered with paper. The interior is peaceful, occupied by the Old Tiger Man. How simple and friendly it is, this tiny pavilion with its altar of red silk, its ceiling of dusty pink, its aqua beams, and its lone painting of the hoary old Tiger Man as a tiger cat!

The elder is gracious and his hair as white as a mountain of snow. He leans confidently against his companion, whose green and fiery iris endows him with a tigerish air altogether at odds with his gentle, catlike charm. Seated among the pines at the foot of a waterfall, the Old Man cools himself with a feather fan.

Since the Koreans have always gone into the mountains searching for the root of life—ginseng—they had good reason to fear the big cats. The holy terror these engendered made the human population want to conciliate the Spirit of the Mountain. They imagined him as an old man whose magic tamed the dark forces and transformed the tiger into his mount.

> *One day four old men were reunited.*
> *Three sat around a jar of vinegar*
> *Into which they dipped a finger to taste its flavor.*
> *One found it bitter, the other sour.*
> *The third thought it sweet.*
> *The fourth, hoary like the snow mountain,*
> *Leaning on his friend the Tiger,*
> *Kept himself apart,*
> *And also took a taste from his jar.*
> *It was a* kimtchi *jar.*
> *Of the three, the first was Gautama,*
> *The second Confucius,*
> *The third was Laocius.*
> *As for the last, they say*
> *History has no name.*
> *He was the Old Tiger Man.*

Captions

The Korean Seasons

1. The symbol of the Supreme Pole uniting *yin* and *yang*, the two complementary aspects of universal harmony.

2. Peasant on the cherry-lined road to Ssangge Temple, the Temple of the Two Valleys.

3. Portrait of master artist Yi Tong Yon of Tamyang, a specialist in painting on bamboo.

4. A peasant visiting the Temple of the Golden Mountain at Kumsan when the magnolia is in flower.

5. The Perfect Pavilion silhouetted against light and a background of poplars and pines somewhere in the southern province of Cholla.

6. Pine forest in the Southern Mountains near Kyongju.

7. In the village of Unsan near Puyo, a pair of peasants who have come to attend a shamanist ceremony.

8. A young porter loaded with bamboo baskets on his way to market in Tamyang.

9. Tamyang's bamboo market.

10. Waterlilies in a pond.

11. Willow pavilion during the spring rains, somewhere in the northern province of Kyongsang.

12. A country couple at the "Courage of the Dragon" portal during a visit to Toksu Palace in Seoul.

13. Peasants visiting the Temple of the Many Pines in Songgwang.

14. A junk on the Han River near Seoul.

15. Kim Bong Nyong of Wonju, a master in the art of mother-of-pearl inlay.

16. Schoolboys in the Village of the Immortals.

17. Studying *The Book of a Thousand Characters* at the Confucian school in the Village of the Immortals.

18. A bamboo artist in Tamyang.

19. The same artist smoking a pipe on the veranda of his house.

20. A young peasant in the northern province of Cholla.

21. The peasants of northern Cholla milling rice.

22. A peasant of the region near Kyongju.

23. Harvesting rice near Kyongju.

24. Kim Tu Mun, the palmist in the folkloric village of Suwar south of Seoul.

25. A pipe-smoking peasant in his cottage in southern Kyongsang.

26. Entrance to the Hall of Great Perfection in the Confucian school at Kangnung on Korea's eastern coast.

27. Im Chang Sun, Confucianist master at Sudong in the province of Kyonggi.

28. Autumn in the Secret Gardens of Changdok in Seoul.

29. The Pavilion of Sweet Harmony in the Secret Gardens of Seoul's Changdok Palace.

30. A persimmon bouquet in a Korean doorway.

31. Young girl in national costume at one of the portals to Seoul's Naksongjae Palace.

32. Schoolboys at a ceremony in Kyongju.

33. Kwon Tai Yon, a dignitary at the spring ceremony of offering to Confucius at Seoul.

34. Suwon's fog pavilion.

35. Winter fog at Suwon.

36. The airy openness of the traditional Korean house.

37. A Confucian scholar of the Andong region.

38. The Southern Han River near Tanyang during a winter freeze.

39. The Southern Han River near Todam's so-called "Three Rocky Peaks."

40. Rocks in the Sorak range of the Snow Mountains.

41. Light and shadow playing over the Little Diamond Mountains.

The Immortals

42. The triple helix, the dynamic emblem of *yin* and *yang*.

43. Gentlemen in the Village of the Immortals contemplating among the rocks.

44. Gentlemen of the Village of the Blue Crane.

45. Meditating in nature.

46. The bird-feather man in the Village of the Immortals.

47. Chanting a sacred text.

48. Transporting a bag of rice on a *tchige* along the path leading to the Village of the Blue Crane.

49. The traditional forge in the folkloric village of Suwon.

50. In the Village of the Blue Crane, the temple where the religion of the "Heavenly Way" is practiced.

51. A traditional meal in the Village of the Immortals.

52. A young calligrapher in the Village of the Immortals.

53. In the Village of the Blue Crane, the traditional horsehair hat of Confucian Korea and the chignon of married men.

54. Quak Chong Mo, a school master in the Village of the Blue Crane.

55. Sa Un Bong, chief of the Village of the Blue Crane, and his wife.

56. Silhouettes shaded in the Chinese manner on a Korean door stretched with mulberry bark.

57. Two men in conversation on the veranda of the temple in the Village of the Immortals.

58. A basket-maker in the folkloric village of Suwon.

59. Morning prayer in the temple of the Village of the Blue Crane. Plaited is the hair style of young men who have not yet married.

Buddhist Monasteries

60. The symbol of Trirutna, the three treasures of Buddhism: the treasure of the Buddha; the treasure of Dharma (law); and the treasure of Sanyha (community).

61. The Venerable Ku San Sunim, Master of the Nine Mountains, spiritual head of the Monastery of the Vast Pines.

62. Pagoda from the Silla period (57 B.C.–A.D. 918) in the Southern Mountains near Kyongju.

63. Hills and royal burial mounds in the Kyongju region.

64. Entrance to the Monastery of the Vast Pines.

65. A pilgrim monk arriving at the temple.

66. Light playing over the roofs of the monastery at Haein—the Monastery of the Ocean Insignia.

67. Drum call at dawn in the monastery.

68. Autumn light and colors on walls and roofs.

69. For the novices of the monastery, the daily labor of sweeping up.

70. Setting the table for a ritual meal.

71. The ritual meal taken by the monks of the Monastery of the Vast Pines.

72. A Buddhist pilgrim timing his prayers by the dull sound of the moktak, a musical block of wood that is struck with a small stick.

73. Playing paduk, a variation upon the Japanese go.

74. The first snow of the winter on the roof of the Monastery of the Ocean Insignia.

75. The library of the Monastery of the Ocean Insignia, which since 1398 has preserved the 81,000 engraved wooden blocks needed to print the sacred texts of Buddhism.

76. The martial arts practiced by the disciples of Master Yang Ik at the Hermitage of the Blue Lotus.

77. Master and disciple in a hermitage.

78. Ashen light over Korea's mountains of the Soraks interior.

1

8

9

11

13

19

20

30

41

42

43

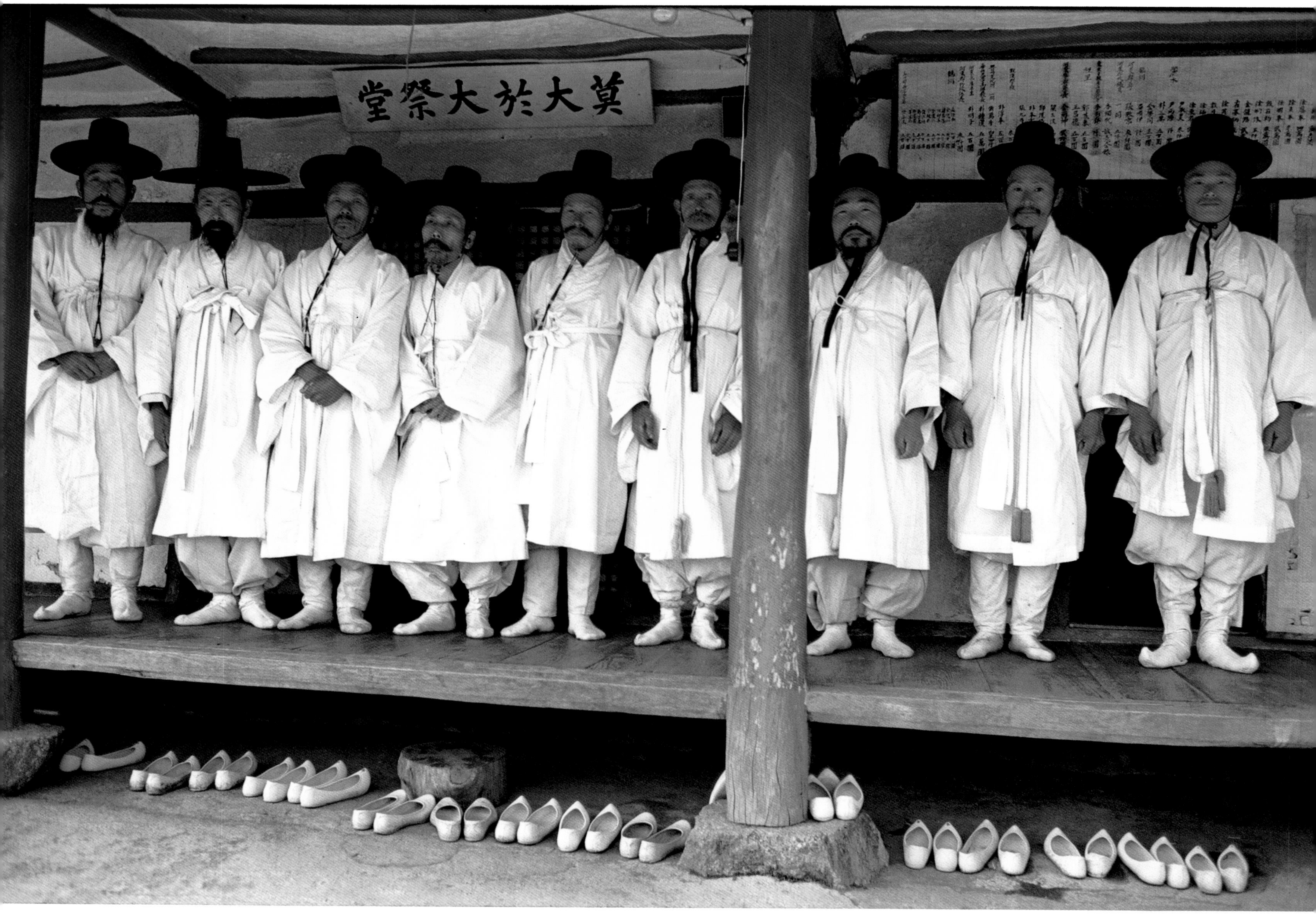
莫大於大祭堂

53

57

58

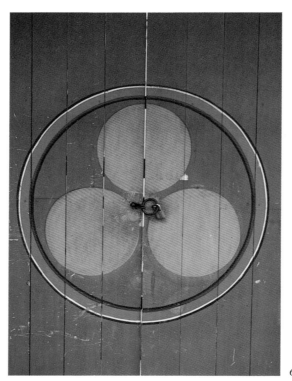

60

61

72

290%

7/28